WITHDRAWN

Take Action

SOCIAL JUSTICE

How You Can Make a Difference

by Lynn Bogen Sanders

Consultant: Adam Fletcher
Director, The Freechild Project
Olympia, Washington

Capstone press®
Mankato, Minnesota

Snap Books are published by Capstone Press,
151 Good Counsel Drive, P.O. Box 669, Mankato, Minnesota 56002.
www.capstonepress.com

Library of Congress Cataloging-in-Publication Data
Sanders, Lynn Bogen.
    Social justice : how you can make a difference / by Lynn Bogen Sanders.
    p. cm. — (Snap books. Take action)
    Includes bibliographical references and index.
    Summary: "Describes what social justice activism is and serves as a guide explaining how youth can make change in their
world" — Provided by publisher.
    ISBN-13: 978-1-4296-2798-6 (hardcover)
    ISBN-10: 1-4296-2798-0 (hardcover)
    1. Social justice — Juvenile literature. 2. Social action — Juvenile literature. 3. Political participation — Juvenile literature. I. Title.
II. Series.
 HM671.S27 2009
 303.3'72 — dc22
                                                   2008027660

Editor: Jennifer Besel
Designer: Veronica Bianchini
Photo Researcher: Wanda Winch
Photo shoot scheduler: Marcy Morin

Photo Credits: All photos by Capstone Press/Karon Dubke, except:
AP Images/Gunnar Ask, 5 (bottom)
Courtesy of Adam Fletcher, 32 (bottom)
Courtesy of Annie Wignall, www.carebags4kids.org, 21
Courtesy of Bilaal Rajan, Handsforhelp.org, 25
Courtesy of Free the Children, www.freethechildren.com, 5 (top), 7
Courtesy of Lynn Sanders, 32 (top)
Courtesy of Rachel Rosenfeld, 17 (both)
Courtesy of Tara Suri, www.aandolan.org, 11

Essential content terms are **bold** and are defined at the bottom of the page where they first appear.

1 2 3 4 5 6 14 13 12 11 10 09

Table of Contents

FREE TO MAKE
A DIFFERENCE

As 12-year-old Craig Kielburger reached for the newspaper comics, he had no idea his life was about to change. Instead of the comics, Craig's eyes fell on the picture of 12-year-old Iqbal (ik-BAHL) Masih.

At the age of 4, Iqbal had been sold into slavery in Pakistan. He was forced to work 12 hours a day tying small knots in carpets at a factory. Iqbal could not go out to play or go to school. If the child workers even spoke to each other, the guards would hit them. The children would be beaten or hung upside down if they became sick or talked back.

When Iqbal was 10, he escaped and began telling people about child slavery. But leaders in the carpet industry didn't like him telling people about this secret. As he became well-known, Iqbal started to receive death threats. But he refused to stop spreading his message. At the age of 12, Iqbal was killed. No one is sure who shot Iqbal. Many people believe the leaders of the carpet industry had him killed because he spoke out.

Craig realized Iqbal's life was very different from his own. But they were the same age. Craig wondered how many other kids were forced to live like Iqbal. And he wondered if a boy in Canada could do anything to help other kids halfway around the world.

When Craig learned about Iqbal, he knew he wanted to do something to help.

Craig Kielburger

Iqbal Masih

Craig went to the library and gathered all the information he could. He discovered that 250 million children worldwide are forced to work as slaves. Craig told his friends about the child workers. They decided to try to help. They named their group Kids Can Free The Children.

The group started small. They put together **petitions**. They also held bake sales and car washes to raise money to fund their project.

A year after starting the group, Craig decided to meet the child workers he was trying to free. With the help of human rights activist Alam Rahman, Craig traveled to south Asia. He met child workers and learned of the horrible jobs they had to do. While in India, Craig held a press conference. He told the world media that Free The Children was working to help the child workers. News stories about Craig and his group played all around the world.

At the age of 13, Craig was talking with world leaders. He learned that child labor began because poor families had no other way to make money. Free The Children began the Adopt a Village program. Through the program, volunteers raise money for different parts of a village's development. They buy a milking animal to provide income. Another option is to raise money to buy bricks for a school. Money raised can also go toward providing clean water. Today, instead of working, 50,000 more children around the world go to school. And more than half of the money raised for Free The Children is from kids under 18. Craig's idea has turned into a huge network of kids helping other kids.

petition – a letter signed by many people asking leaders for a change

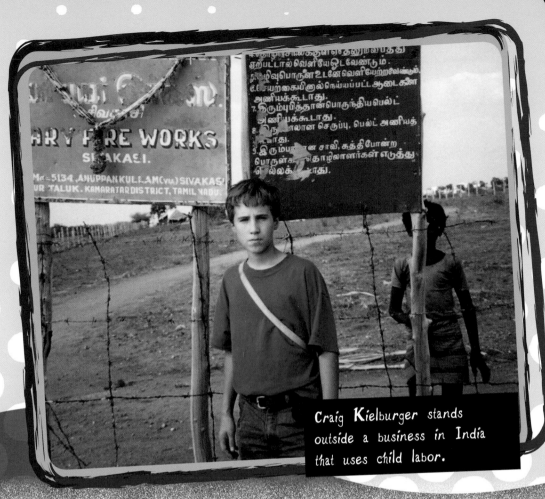

Craig Kielburger stands outside a business in India that uses child labor.

You Can Too!

Being an activist means doing something to make change. An activist for social justice focuses on making life better for other people. Social justice is the idea that every person should have fair and equal rights, like having a safe place to live or being able to go to school. Some activists, like Craig, choose to help others who live far away. Other activists tackle problems like homelessness or hunger right in their own towns. You can work toward social justice too. Ready to get started?

GETTING STARTED

STEP 1: BRAINSTORM PROBLEMS

The first step to making change is finding a problem you want to fix. Start by grabbing a notebook and a pencil. Write down any social problems you can think of. Take a look around your own world. Are there students who need help at school? Maybe you have family or friends who need help. Are there homeless people in your town?

Ideas for problems can be global issues too. News reports about refugees might spark an idea. Maybe a school unit on immigration gets you thinking. It doesn't matter if a problem is big or small — it's important. Write all your ideas down. Don't stop to think about how you'll solve them. Just list the problems you see in the world.

Rules and Regulations

As you're brainstorming, also consider the rules or laws that govern the way people live. Are there any rules you think are unfair to a certain group of people? Or maybe there are laws you think could help others. Consider every possibility, and write it all down.

STEP 2: BRAINSTORM IDEAS AND PICK A CAUSE

Step 2 takes the brainstorming a bit further. Take a look at your list of concerns. For every problem, write down ways you could solve it. For example, say you're concerned about the lack of education for the poor. A list of solutions might look like this:

- Develop teacher workshops that focus on educating at-risk youth.
- Open a tutoring center for poor children with volunteers from the community.
- Hold a school supplies drive to collect pencils and notebooks for needy children to use when they go to class.

Don't judge your ideas. Write down the small ideas and the big, crazy ones. When you brainstorm, you're giving your brain permission to explore. You never know what you'll uncover.

Pick Your Cause

Once you have your list of problems and solutions, it's time to choose where to focus your energy. Look over your list of problems. What issue really touches your heart? Pick something you truly care about. You're going to spend a lot of time working with this issue.

It may be that there are many issues that you care about. Just choose one. You don't want to take on so much that you don't have a clear direction. Remember you can always come back to this list later and tackle a new problem.

Tara Suri was 13 years old when her family took a trip to India. While she was there, Tara was shocked by all the poverty that surrounded her. She was especially worried about the children who had no homes, no food, and no education. Tara decided to help.

At home in Scarsdale, New York, Tara started an organization called HOPE (Helping Orphans Pursue Education). Her goal was to raise money that would improve education for kids in India and Sudan. She started with small actions. She held bake sales, sold bracelets, and recycled soda cans. The money and awareness began to build. Through HOPE, Tara raised $20,000. The money was used to build a dormitory for students to live in at an orphanage in India. HOPE has provided uniforms for students in Sudan. The money has also paid for medical care for students.

But Tara didn't stop there. As her actions grew, so did her organization. Tara created a new organization called Aandolan. Through Aandolan, Tara now runs HOPE and another program called Turn Your World Around. Turn Your World Around is an online resource to help other youth take action. Tara hopes to inspire other kids to make their own social change.

Tara Suri (back right)

CHAPTER 3

LEARN **ALL** ABOUT IT

STEP 3: RESEARCH, RESEARCH, RESEARCH

Ready to support an issue? Great! But before you get out there to take action, you need to do your homework. Gathering all the facts about your issue is one of the most important parts of being an activist. If a reporter asks about your cause, you'll need to be able to answer with the right information. If you're trying to gain support, you'll need facts to back up your position. Step 3 is all about becoming an expert on your cause. It might be tempting to skip this step and get right to work. But later on, that information will be really helpful. You'll be glad you took the time to do the research.

Other Opinions

As you're researching, you will probably come across people with different ideas. Some people might disagree with your point of view. Even your best friend might have a different opinion than yours. That's okay. Take the time to listen to those other views. If you understand what others believe, you might be able to make a stronger case for your ideas. Be respectful of other opinions too. You'll always build more support with a positive, open mind.

There might be times when another opinion makes you change your mind. That's okay too. Step 3 is about learning all you can. You didn't have all the facts when you made your list of problems and solutions. With good information, you'll have opinions supported by facts.

To the Library

One of the easiest places to collect information is at your library. Ask a librarian for help locating books, films, newspapers, and magazines about your topic. Then read or watch them all. Take notes on what you learn. And always jot down where you found the information. Also, keep track of any names, phone numbers, or e-mail addresses you come across. You might want to contact those people later.

Only Online

Another great place to get information is online. Organizations might have Web sites with ideas on how to take action. Research centers might have **statistics** you can use to make your point. You might even find podcasts or videos about your topic. Read or watch these things and soak in all the information. Bookmark good sites so you can come back to them later.

Tip After you do an interview, send a thank-you note. It shows your appreciation, and the person will be more likely to help you in the future.

statistic — a fact shown as a number

The Power of People

In your research, you will probably come across others who know a lot about your topic. Some people might be activists like you. Others might be experts in a related field. All these people can offer you different points of view. You could talk to the coordinator at the local food shelf. Try contacting people at the Red Cross or someone from an activist organization too.

Before you interview someone, be sure to plan ahead. Have some questions ready to ask. Ask your contact about their opinions and actions. See if they know of new resources on your issue. Tell them about your ideas and listen to theirs. Most of all, be polite. Even if you don't agree with their opinions, be respectful of their time.

People at the local food shelf might be able to tell you how many people need food in your area.

Question It

Once you have completed your research, you'll want to study it carefully. Some of the information you find might not be completely accurate. Sometimes people **manipulate** information to support their ideas. Unless you question the facts you're getting, you won't know if you have the truth. Here are some questions to ask yourself as you review your research.

Is the information coming from a trusted **source**? Blogs and wikis can be written by anybody. You don't know why the writers posted the information or even where they got their information. Research centers, nonprofit organizations, or universities are usually more trustworthy places to go for facts.

Is the information based on stereotypes? Stereotypes are broad statements about an entire group of people. But no two people are exactly alike, so stereotypes are never completely true. If you see an article that says, "all homeless people are high school dropouts," you should question that statement.

Does the information seem incomplete? Unfortunately, some pieces of information will not give you all the facts. Some people will leave information out if it doesn't support their ideas. Good resources will tell you about all sides of an issue. If your information only talks about one way to solve a problem, it's not giving you all the facts.

manipulate — to change something in a clever way
source — someone or something that provides information

Rachel Rosenfeld was so sick that she missed an entire year of school. But this 17-year-old didn't let her illness stop her from helping others. While she was sick, Rachel read about teenage girls in Cambodia who were sold by their families for money. She also learned that girls who went to school were sold less often. From her home in Harrison, New York, Rachel went online to do more research. She learned that a Cambodian school could be built for $13,000. Rachel set a goal — she was going to build a school.

Rachel wrote hundreds of letters and sent them to people all across the United States. She asked for donations to help build a new school in Cambodia. She also got support from the World Bank and the Asian Development Bank. Rachel raised $52,000.

Rachel's school was built in Srah Khvav, Cambodia. Now 300 students there have the opportunity for a good education. And Rachel proved that young people can make a big difference.

Rachel Rosenfeld

17

PLANNING

STEP 4: SET A GOAL AND MAKE A PLAN

By now, you've made your lists and picked a cause. And you've become an expert on your topic. Now what? Now it's time to make a detailed plan. First you need to write down your goal. Be specific. A goal to bring peace to all countries of the world is too big. If you want to rebuild a school that was destroyed by war, people will understand your goal.

The next part is to create your plan of action. In Step 4, you'll spell out how you're going to achieve your goal. Don't hesitate to ask for help.

Here are some questions to answer when you make your plan:

- Whom can you contact for help?
- What are you doing? Will you serve food at a shelter? Do you plan to join a club and raise money for children in Africa? Will you go on a trip to build homes in China?
- When are you going to do this, and how long will it take? If your goal is to build a new playground for kids, your plan could take months. It's good to know up front that you could be planning this for a long time.
- Where are you going to do this? Will you need permission from community leaders or even other governments?
- Why are you taking this course of action over another? Why do you think this is the best way to achieve your goal?
- How? Plan your action step-by-step. Figure out the items you need or the advertising you'll do. Outline how many people you'll need to work.

Tip Stay organized. Get a notebook or binder to use just for your activist work. That way you'll be able to find your information when you need it.

Useful You

As you're making your plan, consider the things that you are good at or enjoy doing. If you don't like getting your hands dirty, digging a well probably isn't for you. If you like

working with kids, you could open a tutoring center. Do you like reading? Share stories with the elderly. Are you great on the Internet? Then build a Web site to raise awareness. Use your talents to help someone else. Social justice can be big or small. No matter what you plan to do, you'll be taking action.

Consider the Risk

With any new idea, you can expect challenges. Taking action for social justice could involve a risk. If you question a company's use of child labor, be prepared for the company's reaction. Its leaders might challenge your claims. If you're planning to visit another country, your family might worry about your safety. Before you act, consider the risks involved.

Some risks are fine to take. But if your ideas could hurt or scare people, your plans probably won't work. Before you take action, make sure your risks are necessary. If you're not sure, talk with friends or family. They might be able to help you figure out if your plan will help you reach your goal.

When Annie Wignall was 11 years old, her mom told her something that got her thinking. Her mom said many kids have to leave their homes during a crisis and leave all their things behind. Some of them don't even have a toothbrush. Annie was shocked.

Annie decided that she would help the kids in need. She started Care Bags in her home in Newton, Iowa. First Annie went to local children's agencies. She asked if they would give out the bags. They agreed. So Annie met with business owners and asked for donations. She also found volunteers to sew the bags.

At first, the goal was 20 bags a month. She filled bags with toothbrushes, shampoo, books, and many other items. Soon Annie's work was featured on the news. Requests poured in from people needing help and those wanting to volunteer. Through Airline Ambassadors, her bags are now delivered to kids around the world. Annie's company is still run entirely by volunteers. They send Care Bags to more than 1,000 kids every year.

Annie Wignall

crisis — a time of danger or difficulty

CHAPTER 5

TAKE ACTION!

STEP 5: PUT YOUR PLAN INTO ACTION

You've got your goal and your plan. Now it's time to bring your ideas to life. Step 5 is all about getting out there and making your change happen. Start with getting others involved. You don't have to do it all yourself. Friends and family are a good place to begin. Be enthusiastic and tell them about your plan. Once they are on board, give them a job to do. If your cousin is an artist, have her design a logo. If your brother is good with people, ask him to gather signatures for a petition.

Next branch out and talk to people you don't know. Talk to kids at school and form a club. Hold a rally in your town to let the community know what you're doing. Ask companies in your area to help you by donating money or time. No matter what you do, you're taking action.

Tip Remember a positive attitude makes a difference in everything you do. People are more likely to get involved if they sense your excitement.

Get Out There

To reach your goal, people will need to know about you and your plan. There are many ways to do this. You could put your idea on a flyer and hand it out door-to-door. Create a blog or Web site so others can read your opinions and even write back to you. You could also wear your message on a T-shirt or hat.

Another really powerful way to spread the word about your actions is to contact the media. Reporters are always interested in stories about kids making change. Contact TV and radio stations, and let them know where you'll be and what you're doing. Call up the local newspaper and offer to do an interview. You never know — you might just be the top story on the local news.

Tip Tackling a big goal can be overwhelming. Try doing one thing for your cause each day, and it will feel more manageable.

Bilaal Rajan of Toronto, Canada, has been taking action since he was 4 years old. For Bilaal, activism isn't just a project, it's a way of life. Bilaal's first project began in 2001. He had heard about an earthquake in India. With his grandfather's help, Bilaal raised $350 for earthquake victims by selling oranges door-to-door. Later Bilaal learned about hurricane victims in Haiti and decided to sell cookies at school recess. This time he teamed up with schoolmates, built a Web site, and sold more than 1,000 boxes. His check to UNICEF was for $6,387. But Bilaal didn't stop there. With UNICEF Canada, he started the Canada Kids Earthquake Challenge to aid tsunami victims in southeast Asia. Bilaal personally raised $50,000.

Today Bilaal has his own organization called Hands for Help. Through Hands for Help, he continues to raise money to help children and families throughout the world.

Bilaal Rajan (front right)

Change with Every Step

Change won't happen overnight. It might take a long time to achieve your goal, and it will take a lot of work.

Sometimes activists don't reach the goals they set. Maybe they couldn't raise enough money to build a homeless shelter. Maybe they couldn't stop child abuse. If this happens to you, don't stop taking action.

If you helped even one child, raised one dollar, or spent time making one person a little bit happier, then you have done something great. All change starts with small steps. And all it takes is one person to improve the world. That person is you!

RESOURCES

There are hundreds of resources that can help you be a social justice activist. Below is a short list to help you get started in your research. But don't stop with this list. Find your own resources that will help you reach your goal.

American Civil Liberties Union

The mission of the American Civil Liberties Union is to defend the freedoms that are guaranteed by the U.S. Constitution and Bill of Rights. The ACLU works with U.S. citizens who believe their rights have been taken away. The ACLU has more than 500,000 members. ACLU lawyers work on almost 6,000 court cases every year.

Amnesty International

Amnesty International works to protect the human rights of people all over the world. Members investigate and expose abuses and educate the public. Amnesty International members try to influence governments by lobbying, holding demonstrations, and campaigning online.

Children's Defense Fund

The Children's Defense Fund is a nonprofit organization that focuses its work on helping children. CDF members provide support for children in poverty and other at-risk youth. CDF members also lead programs to help kids grow into healthy adults.

The Freechild Project

The Freechild Project is a program that provides tools, training, and advice to youth activists. The project's Web site offers information on a variety of issues and actions. There are many free resources and ideas for youth to use to work toward change in their worlds.

Human Rights Watch

Human Rights Watch is an organization dedicated to protecting human rights around the world. Members investigate human rights abuses and publish their findings in books and reports. The publicity puts pressure on abusers to change. Members also meet with government officials to help change policies that take away human rights.

Peace Corps

The Peace Corps is an agency of the U.S. government. Peace Corps volunteers work in 74 countries to help people in a variety of areas. The agency's goal is to promote peace and understanding between the United States and the host nations. Volunteers teach English, open computer centers, and raise disease awareness, among many other things.

United Nations Children's Fund

Operating in more than 150 countries, the United Nations Children's Fund is one of the largest supply networks in the world. UNICEF provides education, food, medical care, and other services to needy children around the world.

WireTap Magazine

WireTap is an online magazine for young people who want to create social change. The focus is on news and culture. Topics covered include politics, racial justice, war and peace, education, and the environment.

Glossary

brainstorm (BRAYN-storm) — to think of many ideas without judging them as good or bad

crisis (KRYE-sis) — a time of danger or difficulty

immigration (im-uh-GRAY-shun) — the act of moving to another country to live permanently

manipulate (muh-NIP-yuh-late) — to change something in a clever way to influence people to do or think how you want

petition (puh-TISH-uhn) — a letter signed by many people asking leaders for a change

refugee (REF-yuh-jee) — a person who is forced to leave his or her home because of war or natural disaster

source (SORSS) — someone or something that provides information

statistic (stuh-TISS-tik) — a fact shown as a number or percentage

Read More

Dudley, William, ed. *Social Justice: Opposing Viewpoints*. Opposing Viewpoints. Farmington Hills, Mich.: Greenhaven Press, 2005.

Kielburger, Marc, and Craig Kielburger. *Take Action! A Guide to Active Citizenship*. Hoboken, N.J.: John Wiley & Sons, 2002.

Lewis, Barbara A. *The Teen Guide to Global Action: How to Connect with Others (Near and Far) to Create Social Change*. Minneapolis: Free Spirit, 2008.

Internet Sites

FactHound offers a safe, fun way to find educator-approved Internet sites related to this book.

Here's what you do:

1. Visit *www.facthound.com*

2. Choose your grade level.

3. Begin your search.

This book's ID number is 9781429627986.

FactHound will fetch the best sites for you!

Index

Meet the Author

Lynn Sanders enjoys being an activist and feels passionately about social justice. Her activities include playing music for seniors, raising money for various causes, sponsoring children, and creating awareness about hospital safety. Lynn serves as president of Park Avenue Productions, where she helps nonprofit companies spread their stories through films, written material, teleseminars, and speeches.

Meet the Consultant

Adam Fletcher is a private consultant who has worked with thousands of youth and adults, teaching them how to share their energy and wisdom with each other. He started The Freechild Project to share resources with kids on how to change the world. He also created SoundOut to teach people in schools how to listen to student voice.